WISHES AND WORRIES

COPING WITH A PARENT WHO DRINKS TOO MUCH ALCOHOL

Presented by the Centre for Addiction and Mental Health

Illustrated by LARS RUDEBJER

TUNDRA BOOKS

Published in Canada by Tundra Books,
75 Sherbourne Street, Toronto, Ontario M5A 2P9

Published in the United States by Tundra Books of Northern New York,
P.O. Box 1030, Plattsburgh, New York 12901

Library of Congress Control Number: 2011922896

Library and Archives Canada Cataloguing in Publication
Wishes and worries : coping with a parent who drinks too much alcohol /
presented by the Centre for Addiction and Mental Health ; illustrated by Lars Rudebjer.
(Coping)
ISBN 978-1-77049-238-7
1. Children of alcoholics. 2. Alcoholics–Family relationships.
I. Rudebjer, Lars, 1958- II. Centre for Addiction and Mental Health III. Series: Coping (Tundra Books)
HV5132.W58 2011   362.292'3   C2011-901231-6

We acknowledge the financial support of the Government of Canada through the Book Publishing
Industry Development Program (BPIDP) and that of the Government of Ontario through
the Ontario Media Development Corporation's Ontario Book Initiative. We further acknowledge
the support of the Canada Council for the Arts and the Ontario Arts Council for our publishing program.

A Pan American Health Organization /
World Health Organization Collaborating Centre

Medium: Watercolor and ink on paper
Development: Susan Rosenstein, CAMH; Kathy Lowinger, Tundra Books;
Lauren Bailey, Tundra Books; Jennifer Lum, Random House; Lars Rudebjer

Printed and bound in China

1 2 3 4 5 6   16 15 14 13 12 11

ACKNOWLEDGMENTS

Centre for Addiction and Mental Health Project Team
Susan Rosenstein, MA Project Leader and Product Developer, Publishing Department, CAMH; Bruce Ballon, B.Sc. M.D. E.S.P. (C) FRCP(C), Assistant Professor of Psychiatry, University of Toronto, Head, Adolescent Clinical and Educational Services (A.C.E.S.) for Problem Gambling, Gaming and Internet Use, CAMH; Colleen Kelly, MSW, RSW; Social Work Chief, CAMH; Sharon Labonte-Jaques, Southwestern Ontario Area Manager, Provincial Services, CAMH; Joanne Shenfeld, MSW, R.S.W.; Manager, Family Services and Youth Addictions and Concurrent Disorders Services, CAMH

Special thanks to the following professionals who reviewed early versions of this book, provided invaluable insight and feedback on text and illustrations, and facilitated reviews by families:
Mary Austin, Administrative Secretary, CAMH; Kirstin Bindseil, Advanced Practice Clinician, Day/Residential Program, CAMH; Joanne Brown, Program Director, Parent Action on Drugs (PAD), Toronto, Diane Buhler, Executive Director, Parent Action on Drugs (PAD), Toronto, Gloria Chaim, Project Manager, Pathways to Health Families, The Jean Tweed Centre, Toronto, Diana Dickey, Pathways to Healthy Families, The Jean Tweed Centre, Toronto, Barb Farkus, Addiction Counsellor, Women's Day/Residential Program, CAMH; Jane Fjeld, Youth Priority Knowledge Exchange Manager, CAMH; Lew Goulding, Manager of the Substance Abuse Program for African Canadian and Caribbean Youth (SAPACCY), CAMH; Larry Grand, Project Consultant, CAMH; Julia Greenbaum, Publishing Developer, CAMH; Dennis James, Deputy Clinical Director, Addictions Program, CAMH; Andrew Johnson, Publishing Developer, CAMH; Karen Leslie, MD, FRCPC, Staff Paediatrician, Division of Adolescent Medicine, The Hospital for Sick Children and University of Toronto, Toronto, Katherine Lo, Administrative Secretary, CAMH; Drupati Maharaj, Diversity Knowledge Exchange Manager, CAMH; Geetha Manohar, Administrative Secretary, CAMH; Lisle McGuigan, Early Childhood Development Consultant—Infant Toddler Specialist, Pathways To Healthy Families, The Jean Tweed Centre, Toronto, Lynn McGuigan, Independent Author, Toronto, Ishwar Persad, Education and Training Specialist, Diversity Trainer, CAMH; Dr. David Wolfe, RBC Chair in Children's Mental Health, CAMH

We always open family presents the night before our birthdays, and last year when my turn came, I was excited and happy. That is, until Dad stumbled his way to the couch. He fell asleep before I could open the first present. Instead of good wishes, all I got from him were loud snores. I could tell he'd been drinking.

"Dad bought you a new bicycle," Mom said. "It's bright green. Let's go out and see it."

"I want to see it with Dad! Can't you wake him up? I miss him when he doesn't do things with us."

"You know he'll just be grumpy and angry, Maggie. Come on, don't be sad!"

A bike's a big present, but I'd much rather have had a little present if Dad had only cared enough to give it to me himself.

"What are you going to wish for when you blow out the candles on your cake?" my brother, Daniel, whispered. Daniel is usually really quiet so that Dad doesn't have a reason to yell at him.

I didn't really have to say that all I wanted was for Dad to stop drinking because I knew we all wished that.

Mom bustled around the kitchen.

"Hurry up and finish breakfast, kids," she said. "There's a lot to do before Maggie's party. Beth, can you finish the loot bags while I make the potato salad? Daniel, if you'd walk Candy, it would be a real help."

"I'll pick up the birthday cake," Dad offered.

Mom looked as worried as I felt.

"Are you sure, dear?"

"What's the matter? Do you think I'll let you down?" Dad sounded hurt.

Nobody said a word, but I thought about all the times he had let us down by being late or worse, not even showing up. My stomach was in knots.

Beth, Daniel, and I had just finished decorating the house when the doorbell rang.

I'd invited my friends over, including Amanda. She's my favorite friend from school, but she'd never been to my house. I was too worried about what she'd think of my family.

We played volleyball in the backyard for a while. When it was time to eat, we finished off our hot dogs and potato salad and carrot sticks. Everyone waited for the cake.

"It's okay," said Amanda. It was as though she had read my mind. "I don't think I could eat another bite!" No wonder she's my friend.

It seemed like forever, but Dad finally arrived wearing a silly smile – with the ice-cream cake. He walked unsteadily inside to the kitchen. We all watched as the cake slipped from his hands and fell onto Candy's head. Nobody knew what to do, except for Candy. She was busy lapping up the sweet mess.

Mom yelled at Dad, and Dad yelled back. Daniel hid under the table, Beth stormed out, and I was ready to cry. The guests started phoning their parents to pick them up early. When Amanda left, she gave me a sad little hug as she walked out the door.

The next day, I heard kids whispering that my dad was drunk at my party. I was so hurt and angry that I knocked Amanda's lunch box on the floor. Her surprised look made me feel bad, and I started crying.

"What's going on?" said Mr. Hubble. "Amanda, why don't you and the other kids go outside for recess?"

I thought for sure that I'd get in trouble, but I didn't.

"People shouldn't talk behind your back, but you shouldn't knock anyone's lunch on the floor." Mr. Hubble's voice was kind. "I'm certain you know that, Maggie. Can you tell me why you're so angry?"

He wanted to know why I was angry! He was being really nice, and I wanted so badly to talk to someone. Could I trust him? Was he a safe person to talk to? I remembered when my friend Max told Mr. Hubble about his parents' divorce. Max said Mr. Hubble was a great listener.

I took a deep breath. "I got so upset and embarrassed at my birthday party. My friends saw everything, and now they're telling people my dad was drunk. My parents had a big fight. Everything is such a mess." I talked and talked.

Mr. Hubble said, "Maybe your dad does drink too much alcohol, Maggie. Some people who drink too much can't stop, and they end up saying and doing things that hurt the people they love. Sometimes the people who get hurt don't like to talk about it. Does it help now that you've told me?"

I nodded and tried not to cry.

Mr. Hubble's voice was gentle. "Are your worries the reason your report card wasn't as good as it could have been?"

I nodded again and reached for the tissue that Mr. Hubble handed me.

"I think it might help if you talk to Miss Yee. Lots of kids do – she's a great school counselor. There are tons of families like yours."

All the way home, I thought about what Mr. Hubble had said.
I was scared to tell Mom. What if she was mad that I told our
family secrets to my teacher? Mom had enough to worry about.

But she surprised me. "Maggie, I can tell you're upset
about Dad's drinking and what happened at the party. You
should know we both love all three of you, and we're trying to
make things better."

"Would it be okay if I talked to the school counselor, Mom?"

"I think that's a good thing to do. I'm really proud of
you, Maggie."

"You might not be when you see this," I said.

I gave mom my report card. "I'm disappointed, but I understand," she said.

After dinner, while I was doing my homework, I heard Dad crying and throwing things around the living room. I thought he was upset because of my report card. It must be my fault.

The next day at school, I went to see Miss Yee. I asked her the question that troubled me most. "Is it my fault that Dad drinks too much?

"You didn't cause this problem, Maggie," she said, "and it's not your problem to fix. Sometimes you and your brother and sister may feel upset by what's going on at home. It's important to talk to an adult that you trust about your thoughts and feelings."

I thought for a moment. "Like my grandma!" I said. "I can call her whenever I feel like it. And I can also walk next door to our neighbor Melba's house when things are bad at home."

"Those are fine ideas, Maggie. You can also call a kid's help line."

"My mom told me that Dad's father has a problem with alcohol. Does that mean I'll have problems too?" The idea scared me.

"There are lots of things you can do to prevent that. You have so many things in your life that make you happy, like good friends, music, drawing, playing on the basketball team, and singing in the school choir. And most important, you're good at talking about your feelings. You don't need alcohol to make you feel good."

On the way home, I had another horrible thought. What if Mom started to have problems with alcohol too?

That night, when Mom came to say goodnight, I blurted out my question. "Mom, do you think you'll start drinking too much, like Dad does?"

"That's never been a problem for me, Maggie," she said. "I can stop after a drink or two. But I don't drink with Dad, in case he feels tempted to drink, too."

"So people can drink and not have problems?"

"A lot of people do that," she said. "Alcohol is only a problem for some people."

"I don't understand why people would drink when it causes so much trouble."

Mom thought for a moment. "At first, drinking can make people feel happy or more relaxed. They like that feeling. But if you drink too much, you get drunk, and that can make you feel tired, angry, sad, or sick to your stomach. It can even make you feel sick the next day."

A couple of days later, we were having breakfast when
Mom and Dad said they had an important announcement.
Dad cleared his throat.

"We've been to see Dr. Gupta, and she's helping me with my drinking problem. Mom and I are going to work on things together. Dr. Gupta explained that you kids shouldn't blame yourselves for my bad decisions. She also helped me find a counselor for more help." Beth, Daniel, and I looked at each other. Did this mean things would get better around our house?

The months passed, and Dad pretty much stopped drinking.
He started to spend more time with Beth, Daniel, and me.
He even came to my basketball games with the rest of my
family. It felt great to see him clapping for me.

One day, as we walked home from the park, he said "Maggie, I'm really starting to feel better about myself. I didn't even realize my drinking was a problem until your party. Now I know it affects the whole family. I'm trying hard not to drink anymore. I'm sorry for the trouble that I've caused."

Dad held my hand for the first time in a long while.

I thought about the things that had changed since Dad stopped drinking. Daniel wasn't so nervous that Dad would yell at him, and Beth didn't argue all the time. We were doing family things again, and I was doing way better in school. I could study better when I didn't have to worry about helping Dad. It wasn't my problem to solve. I had enough dealing with math!

But just when I thought we were fine, something terrible happened. Mom asked Dad to take out the garbage. He had been drinking again. I guess Dad didn't want to help because he got angry and started kicking the recycle bin, which tipped over my bike. My birthday bike got all scratched and bent.

I went to talk to Miss Yee about how scared I felt.

"I can see you're disappointed and confused and angry, Maggie."

"How could this happen?" I was ready to cry.

"When people are trying to stop drinking, they sometimes slip and start drinking again. It sounds like that's what happened."

"But why did he get so angry and start kicking the garbage cans?"

"When people drink, they can make bad decisions."

Even with the setback, Dad didn't give up trying to stop drinking. His counselor helped him understand that he should work fewer hours, spend more time with the family, and do the hobbies he used to enjoy. He started gardening again.

By my next birthday, we had some of the fruits and vegetables he'd grown – along with cake and ice cream, of course.

When it was time to blow out the candles, I made my usual wish: *Please don't let Dad come home drunk.*

Everyone was smiling as Dad came in, covered in green paint. He was carrying a bright, neon-green helmet with cool racing stripes.

"Let's all go outside," he said.

There in the yard was my bicycle. It was fixed and painted a shiny green. It looked better than ever.

It was a great present. But the best present of all was that Dad hadn't been drinking. There will probably be more ups and downs, but I really hope he can do it. That's my biggest wish of all.

INFORMATION FOR ADULTS

The Centre for Addiction and Mental Health (CAMH) is one of the leading addiction and mental health organizations in North America and Canada's largest mental health and addiction teaching hospital. CAMH provides outstanding clinical care, conducts ground-breaking research, provides expert training, develops innovative health promotion and prevention strategies, and influences public policy at all levels of government. CAMH also develops publications and resources for health professionals, clients, and the public, providing the most extensive and up-to-date information on topics ranging from prevention to treatment of mental illness and addictions, and promoting best practices in the field.

WHY TALK ABOUT A PARENT WHO DRINKS TOO MUCH ALCOHOL?

Children tend to have common questions and fears when someone in their family drinks too much alcohol, especially a parent. Research has shown that good communication within a family is related to a child's ability to make healthy, positive choices in difficult life situations. Good communication contributes to their resilience or ability to cope with adversity.

Children often understand more than you might think. They need to be able to ask questions, even though it's often hard for them to do so. And they need answers to their questions, even though the questions themselves are difficult. The answers must be clear, concise, and appropriate for the child's age and ability to understand. Children need to hear over and over again that the parent's drinking problem is not their fault.

There is also evidence that having a caring, trustworthy, healthy adult in children's lives can help protect children from the negative effects of a parent's drinking. This person may be a grandparent, teacher, aunt/uncle, or parent of a friend. It is all right for children to reach out for help and it's fine for them to talk about their problems.

If the family doesn't talk openly about the drinking problem, it can become the big secret that is never discussed. It's common for kids to worry about whether or not their parent will ever be able to stop drinking, and whether they have somehow caused their parent's drinking. When children don't get accurate information, they often come to their own conclusions. Their ideas may be wrong and frightening.

There is a number of ways you can encourage children to talk about what it's like having a parent with an alcohol problem. If your children are open to talking, this story can be the focal point of your conversation. It can give you ways to explain the alcohol problem. If your children are not open to talking, simply reading the story will let them know that the questions they think about are the same ones that other children have. Talking about these thoughts will likely help them to feel less alone and confused. Over time, they may feel better able to talk about their feelings, fears, wishes and worries.

Remember, encouraging children to start talking to you and others about a parent who drinks too much alcohol is one of the most important things you can do for them.

Note: If a health care provider or a person who performs professional or official duties with children suspects that a parent or guardian's substance use may be physically or emotionally harming his or her child, this person has a legal responsibility to report this to children's protection agencies, such as the Children's Aid Society (CAS). If you are concerned about a person's legal or ethical responsibility, discuss this issue with him or her.